Everyday
Comfort

Everyday Comfort

Meditations for Seasons of Grief

Randy Becton

BakerBooks
Grand Rapids, Michigan

© 1993 by Randy Becton

Published by Baker Books
a division of Baker Publishing Group
P.O. Box 6287, Grand Rapids, MI 49516-6287
www.bakerbooks.com

New paperback edition published 2006

ISBN 978-0-8010-6788-4

Printed in the United States of America

  The Library of Congress has cataloged the original edition as follows:
Becton, Randy
    Everyday comfort: readings for the first month of grief / Randy Becton.
        p.   cm.
    Includes bibliographical references.
    ISBN 0-8010-1066-7
    1. Grief—Religious aspects—Christianity. I. Title.
BV4905.2.B34 1993
242'.4—dc20   93-3971

CONTENTS

Preface   7

Chapter 1 It's Okay to Cry   9
Chapter 2 Does Anyone Understand My Grief?   11
Chapter 3 Make a New and Special Friendship   16
Meditations

Day 1 Survival Is Sure   28

Day 2 Grief Complications You Can Avoid   30

Day 3 When Is It Time to Cry?   32

Day 4 Other Grievers Teach Us   36

Day 5 Facing Your Own Death   38

Day 6 The Many Faces of Grief   40

Day 7 A Set of Goals   42

Day 8 Answers   44

Day 9 Your Special Needs   46

Day 10 Knowing Your Signs of Recovery   48

Day 11 Knowing What Sorrow Means   50

Day 12 Normal Grief and Abnormal Grief   52

Contents

Day 13 Books That Are Easy to Read and Helpful to Those Who Grieve   54

Day 14 Using the Psalms Daily   56

Day 15 Great Saints Faced Despair   58

Day 16 Reaffirm the Center for Your Life   60

Day 17 Your Recovery Will Be Unique to You   62

Day 18 Let Another Person's Faith Stand with You   64

Day 19 The Truth about Partial Truths 66

Day 20 Solitude's Value   68

Day 21 The Horrible Pain   70

Day 22 A Possible Strategy of Satan   72

Day 23 No Condemnation or Judgment   74

Day 24 Do Not Judge Yourself   76

Day 25 Learning from the Darkness of Another   78

Day 26 Understanding Grief   80

Day 27 Getting through Grief   82

Day 28 Four Paths That Delay Grief   84

Day 29 The Intensity of Grief   86

Day 30 What to Do with Time?   88

Conclusion   91

Appendix 1 A Letter to Becky's Father   93

Appendix 2 Preparing for the Holidays   99

Notes   107

PREFACE

*W*hy did I write this book? Because your grief really matters—to God, for sure, but also to me. I do not say, "I know how you feel," but I daresay, "I have felt the numbness, the loneliness, the questions, the emptiness that result from losing someone you dearly love." I would like to be there with you, to sit quietly, to listen. I want to be your brother in your sorrow. I write with confidence that your grief is understood fully by God.

Counselor C. W. Brister is right to observe that "when hearts are broken, persons do not need explanations. They need the healing presence of God."[1] Counselor Larry Crabb correctly says that "people are hurting more deeply than we know."[2]

Real encouragement takes place in your life when you feel understood in your pain and receive loving words and actions that help you experience God's love and healing. Scripture says that encouraging each other is a work that honors God and results in strengthened confidence in God. If this book helps you strengthen your grip on God's love, you will be encouraged.

Your heart at times may say, "I am afraid." I hope you can move to the confidence that responds, "I will not fear." Your heart may on occasion ask, "Why am I forsaken?" But you, through restating God's promise "I am with you," will be equipped to respond, "Yes, you are with me."

1

It's Okay to Cry

*L*ife does go on. Death is not reversible. Persons who have lost loved ones experience the wrenching pain between knowing one reality but desperately craving another reality. To know what is real does not mean to like it or even to be prepared at this moment to accept it. Grievers even may try to undo the reality of a loved one's death. To act this way is understandable and may be necessary before they can finally say good-bye.

Your grief is a bridge between your loss (the now) and the direction in which you grow (the future). I am not saying to you that something good will come out of this, for I do not want to minimize your grief. But soon you will begin to work on two tasks that you will successfully complete when you are ready: (1) your need to disengage or let go, and (2) your need to reattach or reinvest.

In the days, weeks, and months to come, you will try to accept nurture and care from others. While your needs continue to be met, the time is coming when you will reinvest your unique, God-given strengths in living. Leroy Joesten puts it this way: "There is a time to be helped and a time to stand on one's own."[1]

You need to be comforted and supported, but you also need to be gently challenged to confront your grief. Grieving is uniquely personal. No one can do it for you, though those close to you would love to spare you this pain.

God will help you do the work of grieving and he will help you know when to stop grieving. This will occur in his good time. The permanent room in your heart for this sweet sadness will be filled appropriately. Do not worry; you will never forget. Never place less value on your loved one than you do now. The pain stays with you like a scar from a childhood accident but without the power to crush your spirit. When the time comes—and no one knows this timetable—you will be given strength to resume the gift of life but will feel no betrayal or disservice to the memory of your dear loved one.

Allow others to enter into your pain, to try to begin to understand a fraction of your grief. Life is a laboratory for broken lives, in which people learn to share their humanity (and Christians their Christianity) when they hurt together and stand close to each other. We all are brothers and sisters.

2

DOES ANYONE UNDERSTAND MY GRIEF?

When you grieve it really matters. No other human knows the deep ache you experience when you lose your loved one. That person's unique preciousness to you is beyond words, and now your loved one is gone.

All the people who love you try to say the right words. You know they would give anything if they knew what would console you. But deep in your heart you know they can't really console you because they don't really know what you feel and what you need. You are not sure yourself what you need; you only know that you want the one whom you lost. He or she is irreplaceable, and it seems cruel when one of your well-meaning friends tells you that things will get better with time. Maybe time will help, but you certainly don't think so right now, and this gives you no comfort in your present pain.

Your world is upside down. The silence in the house is almost devastating, but you know that creating noise is not the answer.

Friends tell you that you must eat properly. Intellectually you know that, but you simply are not interested in food. They tell you to get some rest. But even when you try, sleep does not come. You want to shout, "Doesn't anyone know that my grief is my fatigue, and sleeping doesn't relieve it?" But you give each the credit for meaning well, for having a generous heart.

Some friends remind you of the "good times" and urge you to dwell on those good times, the years you were blessed to share life with your precious one. But when you try to dwell on the good times—and there were many—you realize they are over, and you find yourself smiling and crying, crying and smiling. This change, this loss, this death hurts. You resent it. You feel powerless to stop the pain. You feel angry. Sometimes you just feel numb.

Wives, have you set the table for two and then suddenly realized what you've done? Have you checked the yard plants and suddenly remembered he probably would have watered them this week? Have you prepared the laundry and thought, "I'd better get his . . ." and then come face-to-face with it again: "He's gone"?

Husbands, do you begin to pray, but then tears come? You want to blurt out to God, "Oh, God, I'm so alone. I miss her so much. Why didn't I go first? Why her, Lord? Why now?" But then you catch yourself thinking, "Maybe I'm blaming God," or, "I should be doing a better job of coping with this loss." After some time passes, even your friends look for signs that you are coping better. They may say, "You're starting to live again," but you know it's not that simple. Sometimes you're all right and sometimes you're like a frightened child. Then you believe that you can't even tell your closest friends when you aren't coping well.

Do any of the above thoughts describe you? Have you spent a lot of time wondering why you are still here, what God could use you for now, especially if you are in your later years? Parents, siblings, children, and close friends all begin the grieving process by honestly acknowledging these thoughts.

Questions You'd Like Better Answers To

Even after your loss you may be burdened by the difficult memory of the suffering that your loved one experienced. You tried to do your best to serve him or her, but you often felt helpless. You watched with deep love but limited ability to comfort and to give meaningful help. The one who meant everything to you needed more than you could offer. So the questions come.

1. *Why did my loved one have to die?* This is the first big question. You try to think, "What could I have done that would have changed the outcome?" And to think of nothing is still no consolation. You perhaps wonder why God did not make your loved one well. You are faced with the choice of trusting God or letting bitterness creep in.

2. *How can I adjust to this loss?* The answer to this question is not simple. But start, please, by giving yourself as much time as you need to adjust. There is no set time when grief must end. You are an individual, and you may have shared the most intimate friendship or part-

nership possible with a human. You will grow sad during events when you would normally be side by side. You will always have occasions when you think, "My spouse or child would have loved this." This sadness is natural, normal, and healthy. You may cry whenever you want to. Don't let anyone, even a friend, make you feel guilty. You must not concern yourself with pleasing others. Do what you need to do, not what anyone, no matter how close, expects you to do. You own your memories, and they are the great museum of your heart and life experiences. Your loved one will always be a vital part of your life. Therefore, don't try to put him or her in the past; let the memories be a blessed presence with you. Remember, the one you lost wants you to love, laugh, serve, cry, and fully participate in life. That person who trusted you is present in your memory and trusts you still. Your happiness was his or her goal. Remember.

3. *How do I relieve the nagging guilt I feel?* My personal experience tells me that, first of all, your loved one knew your limitations and accepted them far more gracefully and kindly than you could. She knew you would have moved heaven and earth to relieve her suffering and restore her health. Why not, right now, accept her understanding? She did not blame you for anything, so forgive yourself. Your loved one wants you to live fully right now, burdened by no regrets about her death. Remember, she loved you, so honor her by living with meaning, not weighed down in regrets.

4. *Why am I still here?* Many who have fully shared life in partnership find it very difficult to focus on a new goal for meeting a fresh day. May I sincerely suggest that someone needs you. I know that is true, because now that you know sorrow deeply you will be able to

enter another's sorrow and lift his spirit. Charles Dickens wisely wrote, "No one is useless in the world who lightens the burden of it for anyone else." God has unique purposes for your days. Great plans? Yes! To smile and touch a human being's life at this point of need and to give him hope are some of the great things God has in mind for you.

A California lady in her seventies lost a great love of her life. She asked, "What use am I now?" I asked her to think about serving in the role of a "wounded healer." A wise man once said, "Whoever among us has, through personal experience, learned what pain and suffering really are . . . belongs no more to himself alone; he is the brother of all who suffer."

I sympathize with your periods of self-pity in the loss of your precious one; but you and I know that a life built on self-pity produces the bitter fruits of resentment, fear, and enormous unhappiness.

Your choices include the consideration that you can make a difference in someone's life. Human grief at the loss of a loved one is expected. But it is unique when you choose to turn your loss into some value, perhaps leading to the lightening of another's dark path. However, this is only possible when you allow God, through his Spirit, to work in you.

3

Make a New and Special Friendship

*T*he book that has helped me more than any other in my seasons of grief is the book of Psalms. I like what Norman Wright says about the psalms: "Many of them reflect the struggle of human loss but give the comfort and assurance that are from God's mercies."[1] I would add that God thought the psalms would help us know him better and ourselves better. So he kept them recorded as Holy Scripture. I have grown to treasure *The Message of the Psalms*, by Walter Bruggemann (Augsburg Press, 1984), *Out of the Depths: The Psalms Speak for Us Today*, by Bernhard W. Anderson (Westminster Press, 1983), and *Insights From the Psalms*, by John T. Willis (ACU Press, 1974), a close personal friend and excellent Bible scholar.

Let me explain why the psalms have become my warm friends and good traveling companions through the rough weather of grief. First, they reflect Israel's faith, which was produced by God's covenant relationship with them. Second, they tell us a tremendous amount about God, his glory, and his intentions toward his creation—humanity. Also, my friend Tony Ash, who co-authored a commentary on the book of Psalms, says that when you get thoroughly familiar with the psalms you can "find balm for every wound." Christians today pray to the same God the Hebrews prayed to, sharing their confessions, feelings, and hopes. Believers see themselves more clearly in Psalms, perhaps, than anywhere else in Scripture.

A number of the psalms are hymns (about forty) that center on praising God. In addition to these loved psalms is another group especially appreciated by hurting people, the psalms known as *individual laments*. Maybe one-third of all psalms take this form. Individual laments are cries to God from people in the worst time of their pain begging for relief. All kinds of trouble exist—illness, losses, hurtful accusations, threats against life, anxiety and worry, poverty, mistreatments, and, of course, fear of death.

In many psalms a problem is specifically addressed, while in others the exact problem is more vague. But the hurting psalmist asks God to hear and care about what's happening to him. Sometimes, when the problem is described, the psalmist gives reasons why God should act, then expresses trust or gratitude for God's concern and action—before or after the fact. You can find a comfortable place in these readings; you are not alone in your sadnesses and problems. More than that, you learn a lot about God through the record of the writers' journeys of faith, of when they were weak and when they were strong. The psalmists are human beings who speak with intensity to God. The following are individual laments: Psalms 3, 5–7, 13, 17, 22, 25, 26, 28, 35, 38, 39, 41–43, 51, 54, 55, 57, 59, 61, 64, 69, 71, 86, 88, 102, 109, 120, 130, 140–43.

But I must quickly add that I also receive comfort in times of grief from psalms of thanksgiving: Psalms 30, 34, 40, 52, 66, 92, 116, 138, and others. These psalms give God praise for deliverance of some kind. They underscore not just a dilemma but God's deliverance and the praise he deserves. And, of course, I often pray the psalms of trust: Psalms 11, 16, 23, 27, 62, 131.

To take my pain to God in confession but then learn to focus my attention less on my pain and more on his grace becomes a unique growth experience in my faith. I hurt myself when I bypass these sources of real comfort (where the Spirit of God is truly present) for something more current but transient. Predictably then I will remain spiritually undernourished and anemic in my faith.

My experience may help you understand how strongly I view the psalms as friends of my spirit and physicians to my soul. When I was desperately ill I couldn't consistently read anywhere else in Scripture but in the book of Psalms. The psalms fed my soul over and over because I was crying out to my God and longed to be heard by him and held close in his strong arms. Again and again I opened the Bible to the psalms. I pitched my tent there and camped there. I was never disappointed. The Lord "heals the broken-hearted and binds up their wounds" (Ps. 147:3). God is very near when a Christian is in sorrow. This is clearly seen in the psalms. Reading Psalms is a health-restoring prescription for grief recovery.

The special psalms of lament are important enough for you to learn to depend on them. When you make a psalm of lament your very own lament you do not declare a lack of faith, but you boldly believe God so that you can tell him exactly how you feel. You trust him with your real self. You cannot pretend but must tell the Father where you hurt.

Some call the psalms of lament psalms of darkness, but it is more important to think of them as prayers addressed to the God who is himself one of sorrows and acquainted personally with grief. He cries with you. But beyond the tears he has the power to transform situations, to bring new hope out of hopelessness and new life out of death. He mends your broken places. Maybe you think God is disappointed in you for crying out when life hurts. But he is not; he is pleased.

A healthy faith requires that you face the dark times and tell the truth. New life from God is possible when pretending stops and reality is confessed. God is the Lord of all human experience, a participant in it. Jesus was called Immanuel, meaning "God with us." The psalmists of lament use strongly stated language because they want God to get involved and change the situation. Life has tumbled in on them, and only God can lift the weight from crushed chests.

In several of these psalms the plea turns into praise because God hears the prayer. God, in a way consistent with his plan and promises, has done something to cause the psalmist to praise him for his faithfulness. The reader of these movements from *plea* to *praise* is strengthened in faith, reassured of God's loving intentions, and does not feel so alone or abandoned. This is illustrated in Psalm 13:

How long, O LORD? Will You forget me forever?
How long will You hide Your face from me?
How long shall I take counsel in my soul,
Having sorrow in my heart daily?
How long will my enemy be exalted over me?

Consider and hear me, O LORD my God;
Enlighten my eyes,
Lest I sleep the sleep of death;
Lest my enemy say,
"I have prevailed against him";
Lest those who trouble me rejoice when I am
    moved.

But I have trusted in Your mercy;
My heart shall rejoice in Your salvation.
I will sing to the LORD,
Because He has dealt bountifully with me.

When the psalmist perceives God's absence he has
pain, sorrow, and, worst of all, a feeling that enemies
have won. The psalmist is overwhelmed. Only God can
help. Then the psalmist must wait, and some time later
he adopts a new outlook, reassured of God's steadfast
love and salvation. He has trusted. He had to wait. Now
he can rejoice and sing.

One of my all-time favorites is Psalm 86:

Bow down Your ear, O LORD, hear me;
For I am poor and needy.
Preserve my life, for I am holy;
You are my God;
Save Your servant who trusts in You!
Be merciful to me, O LORD,
For I cry to You all day long.

Rejoice the soul of Your servant,
For to You, O LORD, I lift up my soul.
For You, LORD, are good, and ready to forgive,
And abundant in mercy to all those who call
    upon You.

Give ear, O LORD, to my prayer;
And attend to the voice of my supplications.
In the day of my trouble I will call upon You,
For You will answer me.

Among the gods there is none like You, O LORD;
Nor are there any works like Your works.
All nations whom You have made
Shall come and worship before You, O LORD,
And shall glorify Your name.
For You are great, and do wondrous things;
You alone are God.

Teach me Your way, O LORD;
I will walk in Your truth;
Unite my heart to fear Your name.
I will praise You, O LORD my God, with all my
    heart,
And I will glorify Your name forevermore.
For great is Your mercy toward me,
And You have delivered my soul from the
    depths of Sheol.

O God, the proud have risen against me,
And a mob of violent men have sought my life,
And have not set You before them.
But You, O LORD, are a God full of compassion,
    and gracious,
Longsuffering and abundant in mercy and truth.

Oh, turn to me, and have mercy on me!
Give Your strength to Your servant,
And save the son of Your maidservant.
Show me a sign for good,
That those who hate me may see it and be
    ashamed,
Because You, Lord, have helped me and com-
    forted me.

The psalmist needs God to listen, take pity, give strength, and save. We don't know his exact problem, only that he really needs God and he needs him now. He rehearses God's uniqueness and is sure God can comfort, for he had done so often enough in the past. In verse 17 the Lord "helped me": help was needed, requested urgently, expected, and thankfully received. The movement of the psalm is from *trouble* to *confidence*.

In a similar vein is Psalm 35:

Plead my cause, O Lord, with those who strive
    with me;
Fight against those who fight against me.
Take hold of shield and buckler,
And stand up for my help.
Also draw out the spear,
And stop those who pursue me.
Say to my soul,
"I am your salvation."

Let those be put to shame and brought to
    dishonor
Who seek after my life;
Let those be turned back and brought to
    confusion
Who plot my hurt.

Let them be like chaff before the wind,
And let the angel of the LORD chase them.
Let their way be dark and slippery,
And let the angel of the LORD pursue them.
For without cause they have hidden their net
for me in a pit,
Which they have dug without cause for my life.
Let destruction come upon him unexpectedly,
And let his net that he has hidden catch himself;
Into that very destruction let him fall.

And my soul shall be joyful in the LORD;
It shall rejoice in His salvation.
All my bones shall say,
"LORD, who is like You,
Delivering the poor from him who is too strong
for him,
Yes, the poor and the needy from him who
plunders him?"

Fierce witnesses rise up;
They ask me things that I do not know.
They reward me evil for good,
To the sorrow of my soul.
But as for me, when they were sick,
My clothing was sackcloth;
I humbled myself with fasting;
And my prayer would return to my own heart.
I paced about as though he were my friend or
brother,
I bowed down heavily, as one who mourns for
his mother.

But in my adversity they rejoiced
And gathered together;
Attackers gathered against me,
And I did not know it;

They tore at me and did not cease;
With ungodly mockers at feasts
They gnashed at me with their teeth.

Lord, how long will You look on?
Rescue me from their destructions,
My precious life from the lions.
I will give You thanks in the great congregation;
I will praise You among many people.

Let them not rejoice over me who are wrong-
    fully my enemies;
Nor let them wink with the eye who hate me
    without a cause.
For they do not speak peace,
But they devise deceitful matters
Against the quiet ones in the land.
They also opened their mouth wide against me,
And said, "Aha, aha! Our eyes have seen it."

This You have seen, O Lord;
Do not keep silence.
O Lord, do not be far from me.
Stir up Yourself, and awake to my vindication,
To my cause, my God and my Lord.
Vindicate me, O Lord my God, according to Your
    righteousness;
And let them not say in their hearts, "Ah, so we
    would have it!"
Let them not say, "We have swallowed him up."

Let them be ashamed and brought to mutual
    confusion
Who rejoice at my hurt;
Let them be clothed with shame and dishonor
Who magnify themselves against me.

Let them shout for joy and be glad,
Who favor my righteous cause;
And let them say continually,
"Let the Lord be magnified,
Who has pleasure in the prosperity of His
    servant."
And my tongue shall speak of Your
    righteousness
And of Your praise all the day long.

The need is desperate. Trouble is right on top of the psalmist and he is not sure he will be able to trust. Despair is not the answer. He asks God for help. Things seem out of control and God should act. In verse 17 he feels God has been absent and slow to respond. Then he promises to praise God, for he is sure God will act. The psalmist knows God keeps his covenant and has always acted to deliver his people. But will God please hurry? The psalmist wants rescue, after which he will praise God for his greatness. The idea here is that God's unique place among the nations, his greatness, will only be praised if he delivers on his promise to act (see vv. 10, 27).

MEDITATIONS

DAY 1

Survival Is Sure

Face the truth that sorrow over your loved one does not mean God has moved away from you. He remains near.

Refuse to worry about excessive self-pity. These feelings are only an expression of your sense of loss and are not permanent.

Feeling painfully alone does not mean you are giving up.

Your spirit, though broken, will not be defeated, for God's plan for you is larger than this terrible loss.

I Feel Extremely Alone

Hear my prayer, O LORD,
And let my cry come to You.
Do not hide Your face from me in the day of my trouble;
Incline Your ear to me;
In the day that I call, answer me speedily.
For my days are consumed like smoke,
And my bones are burned like a hearth.
My heart is stricken and withered like grass.

Psalm 102:1–4

I have become like a lonely bird on a housetop.

Samuel Taylor Coleridge,
"The Rime of the Ancient Mariner"

In high school I felt chills down my spine when I read Coleridge's lyrical ballad, especially these lines:

Alone, alone, all, all alone
Alone on a wide, wide sea!
And never a saint took pity on

My soul in agony. . . .
So lonely 'twas that God himself
Scarce seemèd there to be.

In my own grief I have often felt all alone. Telling myself that I was not alone didn't help much, even though it was true. Remember, David the psalmist felt terribly alone at times, especially during his troubles from Absalom. The same David wrote: "The LORD is my shepherd, I shall not want." Let your brother David remind you that *feeling* alone is not *being* alone.

My loss is all I think about
from early morning to early morning.
Will it ever be different?
In a sense I don't want to
think of anything else—lest
I minimize the beauty of
my loved one's life.
Help me never to forget,
yet to find your way
to live with the pain.

DAY 2

Grief Complications You Can Avoid

Reject making statements like "It's taking me too long to bounce back."

Reject giving a lot of thought to what you could have done to prolong life: "If only I . . ."

Reject focusing blame on a medical person or institution.

Reject developing a secret "I hate God" campaign in your heart, which you mask by church attendance.

God at Work in the Dark

For His anger is but for a moment,
His favor is for life;
Weeping may endure for a night,
But joy comes in the morning.

Now in my prosperity I said,
"I shall never be moved."

Psalm 30:5–6

Eugenia Price, in *Getting Through the Night*, a small, encouraging book on handling grief, writes that the problem is the slow movement from night to morning. Her helpful emphasis is found in this paragraph:

Even in the darkness the God who loves us has been ministering to us without our knowing. It helps if we do know that he has been at work within us through all that black night, but it's all right if we aren't always aware of it . . . and what counts . . . is the fact, the irrevocable, eternal fact, that he knows us.[1]

Remember the one who says, "I am the light of the world." But nights in grief are pitch dark. You are worn out by grief. There is no promise of specific relief, but he knows you and your needs and he cares. God promises that the night of weeping will come to an end. Your chief work right now is to trust him to determine when the end of weeping will come.

> Lord, you brought me to salvation
> through your son.
> You brought me to hope
> through your son.
> You brought me to joy
> through your son.
> Thank you.
> Acquainted with grief, he
> Willingly became my deliverer.

DAY 3

When Is It Time to Cry?

It's time to cry each time you feel emptiness.

It's time to cry when letters come, someone's laugh sounds similar to your loved one's, a favorite soup is cooking but only for one.

It's time to cry when you remember vivid scenes of fun, play, and humor shared.

It's time to cry when you see sickness, limitation, or death in someone's family and you participate in their sadness.

Tears are messages, God's wise way for your grief to be expressed.

Crying is love and hope staying alive through memory.

He Is Totally Dependable

The Lord is my light and my salvation;
Whom shall I fear?
The Lord is the strength of my life;
Of whom shall I be afraid?
When the wicked came against me
To eat up my flesh,
My enemies and foes,
They stumbled and fell.
Though an army should encamp against me,
My heart shall not fear;
Though war should rise against me,
In this I will be confident.

One thing I have desired of the LORD,
That will I seek;
That I may dwell in the house of the LORD
All the days of my life,
To behold the beauty of the LORD,
And to inquire in His temple.
For in the time of trouble
He shall hide me in His pavilion;
In the secret place of His tabernacle
He shall hide me;
He shall set me high upon a rock.

And now my head shall be lifted up above my enemies all
  around me;
Therefore I will offer sacrifices of joy in His tabernacle;
I will sing, yes, I will sing praises to the LORD.

Hear, O LORD, when I cry with my voice!
Have mercy also upon me, and answer me.
When You said, "Seek My face,"
My heart said to You, "Your face, LORD, I will seek."
Do not hide Your face from me;
Do not turn Your servant away in anger;
You have been my help;
Do not leave me nor forsake me,
O God of my salvation.
When my father and my mother forsake me,
Then the LORD will take care of me.

Teach me Your way, O Lord,
And lead me in a smooth path, because of my enemies.
Do not deliver me to the will of my adversaries;
For false witnesses have risen against me,
And such as breathe out violence.
I would have lost heart, unless I had believed
That I would see the goodness of the Lord
In the land of the living.

Wait on the Lord;
Be of good courage,
And He shall strengthen your heart;
Wait, I say, on the Lord!

Psalm 27

On whom can you depend to stay near when you are covered with grief and are no pleasure to be with? My friend David Redding says, "Faith is for those who have sized up their situation as hopeless unless they have heaven's help."[1] The psalmist has experienced God's kindness and wants to stay very close to God. Handling rough times in the future is possible because he has been comforted by God in the past. His confidence in facing the unknown comes from the one who is well known because of what he has done.

Lord, I cannot pray for my frequent crying.
My heart is dark and lonely.
Thank you for not leaving me.
Thank you for your help hour by hour.
Thank you for peace.
Somehow, you will see me through.

DAY 4

Other Grievers Teach Us

Earl Grollman's *What Helped Me When My Loved One Died* offers guidelines based on things that grieving people told him helped them to move from helplessness to hopefulness. Among those things are the following:

Don't compare yourself with others in similar situations. Your own way is the best way for you.

Pick your own times, but leave your house. Take that first step; you won't be bothering a friend you call to be a companion when you go to the store.

Don't rule out a short-term grief support group. Participants have been where you are and tend to be accepting and encouraging.

Grief expert Elisabeth Kübler-Ross writes, "Love as your loved one would have encouraged you and serve others to honor their memory. You'll like the way you feel."

Take out the momentos and smile through the tears. These times belong to you, and you deserve to remember.[1]

He Knows All about You

O LORD, You have searched me and known me.
You know my sitting down and my rising up;
You understand my thought afar off.
You comprehend my path and my lying down,
And are acquainted with all my ways.
For there is not a word on my tongue,
But behold, O LORD, You know it altogether.

Psalm 139:1–4

A church service had not met my needs like this one for a long time. Old Testament scholar John Willis, a specialist on the psalms and a good friend, spoke to the large audience who, he said, "may be especially disheartened today." I thought I qualified.

He began by pointing out that the author of the above verses of Psalm 139 feels misunderstood by everyone on earth. But in God he finds one who understands him completely. And we do too.

Then Dr. Willis summarized verses 7–12: the author feels "I am all alone" but realizes that God is with him.

Another disheartening feeling (see vv. 13–16) is, "I am not beautiful." Then to know that God has uniquely created him brings comfort.

A final discouragement (see vv. 19–22) is the feeling that the wicked win in this world. The writer is filled with anxious thoughts (see v. 23).

As I listened I wondered, "How did the preacher get a page out of my private diary?" He had shown me that my feelings did not match the truth. God understands me. I am not alone. To him I am beautiful. The wicked (and self-destructive thoughts) do not win, and he will lift me out of my despondency.

I'm glad I went to church that Sunday, for the Word of the Lord restored my perspective.

> Sweet Jesus, give me grace
> To cover my fears.
> In the Garden of
> Gethsemane you received
> Comfort and encouragement.
> Console me; calm my heart.

DAY 5

Facing Your Own Death

"So teach us to number our days that we may apply our hearts to wisdom."

Life has greater purpose when you fully appreciate your finitude.

Each loved one you lose prepares you to face your own death.

Making peace with your past (through acceptance of God's grace) is possible in these days.

Your friends and family will be a great source of strength. They are God's gifts to you.

Find your own way to honor the memory of your loved one, for it can bring enormous consolation.[1]

Feeling Forsaken

My God, My God, why have You forsaken me?
Why are You so far from helping Me,
And from the words of My groaning?
O My God, I cry in the daytime, but You do not hear;
And in the night season, and am not silent.

But You are holy,
Who inhabit the praises of Israel.
Our fathers trusted in You;
They trusted, and You delivered them.
They cried to You, and were delivered;
They trusted in You, and were not ashamed.

Psalm 22:1–5

This psalm meant a lot to Jesus and will to you.

It is frustrating to feel that God has let you down, that he doesn't answer when you call on him. Persons of strong faith can still have periods of temptation toward despair. The devil, remember, attacked Jesus in the wilderness. This psalm was used by Jesus and actually bonds you to him.

He wants you to know that faith can be severely bruised without being permanently damaged. You may temporarily lose your way, but your choosing faith lets you persevere. Put your faith not in faith but in God again. Make it your habit to believe again and again. Say with Jesus, "Father, into your hands I commit my spirit."

> Dear Lord, you are with me.
> Through you I survive;
> Without you I sink.
> You carry my broken heart.
> I need you every hour.
> Jesus Christ, thank you for comfort.

DAY 6

The Many Faces of Grief

Frequent periods of anxiety are normal because of the separation caused by death.

Numbness, emptiness, loneliness, and isolation can make even normal tasks such as doing the laundry, grocery shopping, and vacuuming seem impossible to accomplish.

Grief can erupt at awkward moments: at lunch, singing in church, starting your car. Don't be ashamed when your grief does not follow a normal timetable.

Periods of anger toward your loved one, other members of the family, yourself, or God are normal.

Watch out for nighttime. Listen to Job: "My bones are pierced in me at night, and my gnawing pains take no rest" (Job 30:17).

When You Don't Feel It

I have become absolutely convinced that neither death nor life, neither messenger of Heaven nor monarch of earth, neither what happens today nor what may happen tomorrow, neither a power from on high nor a power from below, nor anything else in God's whole world has any power to separate us from the love of God in Christ Jesus our Lord!

Romans 8:38–39 Phillips

J. B. Phillips's brilliant knowledge of Greek led to a bestselling translation of the New Testament. He found deep assurance in his translation of the two verses above. He needed the assurance. He fought a lifelong battle with anxiety and depression even while he was an effective preacher, a bestselling author, and a popular speaker on the British Broadcasting Corporation.

He carried on a heavy load of correspondence with people whose insecurities about God's love and other trials of faith often made them feel left out; they didn't seem to measure up to what others expected of them. He is one of my spiritual heroes, largely because he did not hide his personal struggle and he did not quit.

> Lord, have mercy
> In my hour of trial
> As you had mercy for my sins
> At Calvary.
> My grief numbs me to life's promise.
> Gently lead me back to life.

DAY 7

A Set of Goals

I will not overreact to how I feel or act but will try to understand that I will survive.

I will not hold it all in. I will choose when to involve friends to share this grief.

I will not build my life around this loss, although right now I don't know how to avoid it.

I will seek to be kind, though I pray for a high tolerance from family and friends when I'm blue.

I will keep on believing, though I don't understand God's timing at all. I *believe* the truth of my faith, but I don't fully *feel* this truth right now.

Feelings of Guilt

Blessed is he whose transgression is forgiven,
Whose sin is covered.
Blessed is the man to whom the LORD does not impute
    iniquity,
And in whose spirit there is no deceit.

When I kept silent, my bones grew old
Through my groaning all the day long.
For day and night Your hand was heavy upon me;
My vitality was turned into the drought of summer. Selah.
I acknowledged my sin to You,
And my iniquity I have not hidden.
I said, "I will confess my transgressions to the LORD,"
And You forgave the iniquity of my sin. Selah.

For this cause everyone who is godly shall pray to You
In a time when You may be found;
Surely in a flood of great waters

They shall not come near him.
You are my hiding place;
You shall preserve me from trouble;
You shall surround me with songs of deliverance. Selah.

Psalm 32:1–7

When you grieve the loss of someone, it helps to know your sins are forgiven so that you don't complicate grief with unnecessary guilt. As God's child—washed in the blood of Jesus Christ daily, walking in faith—you can praise God, for you are not guilty.

All are sinners for sure. But through your participation by baptism in the death, burial, and resurrection of Jesus, you receive his salvation by grace. Tell yourself this truth. Praise God. Jesus took your guilt.

Do you have the sweet relief God intends for you? Keep on confessing your sin while you receive his forgiveness, but don't linger in sadness over sin confessed and forgiven. Sing a happy song of deliverance.

> Lord, I am hurting badly,
> Wounded in my spirit,
> Aching every hour.
> Yet, you protect me
> From self-destruction,
> The acts of disbelief, and disobedience.
> I will call upon your name;
> Your strength sustains me
> And keeps me from perishing.
> Your grace wraps me in your
> Warm love.

DAY 8

Answers

Remember that answers are only partial and mostly inadequate when the heart is broken.

Life and loss remain profound mysteries.

Comfort comes from unexpected sources, usually in quiet, simple ways.

The path to survival requires many reminders from the loving, caring God who grieves with you in life's darkest hours.

Your Help and Your Deliverer

I waited patiently for the LORD;
And He inclined to me,
And heard my cry.
He also brought me up out of a horrible pit,
Out of the miry clay,
And set my feet upon a rock,
And established my steps.
He has put a new song in my mouth—
Praise to our God;
Many will see it and fear,
And will trust in the LORD.

Blessed is that man who makes the LORD his trust,
And does not respect the proud, nor such as turn aside to lies.
Many, O LORD my God, are Your wonderful works
Which You have done;
And Your thoughts toward us
Cannot be recounted to You in order;
If I would declare and speak of them,
They are more than can be numbered.

Psalm 40:1–5

God's people, when in trouble, often vowed to God to sing his praises if God would help them. The psalmist waited until God had taken care of him. God is helping you cope. Bless someone near you by telling of God's help. Show God how grateful you are.

> Father,
> Help me run the race;
> Help me finish the course;
> Help me keep the faith.
> Bring me home with you, Father,
> In your own good time.

DAY 9

Your Special Needs

David K. Switzer, a specialist in understanding crises and grief, lists these needs as basic to all grievers:

You need to identify and express your feelings to someone you trust.

You need to be assured how valuable you are.

You need to be sure you have said good-bye to the one you have lost and to learn to love that person in a different way now.

You need to deepen old relationships when possible and be open to the establishing of new ones.

When you are ready you may need to rearrange physical reminders of the one who has died.

Healing and renewal are possible. God will make a way through the pain for you.[1]

A Very Present Help in Trouble

God is our refuge and strength,
A very present help in trouble.
Therefore we will not fear,
Though the earth be removed,
And though the mountains be carried into the midst of the sea;
Though its waters roar and be troubled,
Though the mountains shake with its swelling. Selah.

There is a river whose streams shall make glad the city of
     God,
The holy place of the tabernacle of the Most High.
God is in the midst of her, she shall not be moved;
God shall help her, just at the break of dawn.
The nations raged, the kingdoms were moved;
He uttered His voice, the earth melted.

The LORD of hosts is with us;
The God of Jacob is our refuge. Selah. . . .

Be still, and know that I am God;
I will be exalted among the nations,
I will be exalted in the earth!

The LORD of hosts is with us;
The God of Jacob is our refuge. Selah.

Psalm 46:1–11

I find myself saying often, at times such as while driving or taking a bath, "The Lord is my refuge and strength, my ever-present help in trouble." I feel his nearness. With God near, panic goes away. He is in charge, so I relax and trust him. This psalm connects my heart with these words of Jesus: "Let not your hearts be troubled; you believe in God" (John 14:1). I have nothing to fear.

> Lord, I give you thanks
> For the life of my beloved,
> For the kindnesses you gave us
> Through your mercy,
> For a beautiful human being
> I knew and loved.
> You do everything perfectly, Father.

DAY 10

Knowing Your Signs of Recovery

Dr. William Worden, a grief counselor, spoke recently on "When Is Mourning Finished?" His guidelines indicate there are no easy answers, but he offered these encouragements:

No one can set the time, but in the loss of a close loved one, full resolution through grief probably occurs within two years.

One indicator of recovery is the ability to think of the loved one without great pain, only with a sweet sadness.

Another indicator of recovery is that time when you can reinvest emotions into living.

Some studies have shown that three to four years must pass before emotional pain has gone.

Watch for the way you respond when friends mention your loved one. You will see how well you are adjusting.

Your loss is a permanent part of your life.

Sing for Joy

Oh come, let us sing to the LORD!
Let us shout joyfully to the Rock of our salvation.
Let us come before His presence with thanksgiving;
Let us shout joyfully to Him with psalms.
For the LORD is the great God,
And the great King above all gods.
In His hand are the deep places of the earth;
The heights of the hills are His also.
The sea is His, for He made it;
And His hands formed the dry land.

Oh come, let us worship and bow down;
Let us kneel before the LORD our Maker.
For He is our God,
And we are the people of His pasture,
And the sheep of His hand.

Psalm 95:1–7

Those who grieve discover new truths. They begin to connect pleasure with praise. "But I don't feel like singing about joy in a time of grief," you say. But you may be surprised if you try. By worshiping him, you will find the Lord your maker to be a focus that is larger than your loss.

Thank God in your darkest hour. Read Psalm 103 for help to recall his loving-kindness and tender mercies. Restate his benefits. You will find healing in praise.

Lord,
I ask not
That you take my pain away;
I ask that I be given
Strength to endure
As I move through grief.

DAY 11

Knowing What Sorrow Means

Edgar Jackson wrote: "The ability to mourn may not seem to be a major asset in life. Yet as one of the Beatitudes puts it, 'Blessed are they that mourn, for they shall be comforted.'"[1]

In the J. B. Phillips Version this Beatitude reads: "How happy are those who know what sorrow means, for they will be given courage and comfort" (Matt. 5:4).

Grieving is neither weakness nor lack of power.

The Power of Staying in the Word

Oh, how I love Your law!
It is my meditation all the day. . . .

How sweet are Your words to my taste,
Sweeter than honey to my mouth!
Through Your precepts I get understanding;
Therefore I hate every false way.

Your word is a lamp to my feet
And a light to my path. . . .

Your testimonies I have taken as a heritage forever,
For they are the rejoicing of my heart.
I have inclined my heart to perform Your statutes
Forever, to the very end. . . .

You are my hiding place and my shield;
I hope in Your word. . . .

Uphold me according to Your word, that I may live;
And do not let me be ashamed of my hope.

Psalm 119:97, 103–105, 111–112, 114, 116

Could it be that grievers are malnourished spiritually because they are not in the Word daily? The psalms are not required reading, unless your goal is to survive spiritually. Loneliness dissipates when God is your constant companion. Intimacy with God helps weaken doubt and fear.

Small children sometimes feel secure when they sleep with a stuffed animal. Believers sleep securely with God's presence through his Spirit. One friend says, "When life is too much for us, it is time to get lost in wonder, love, and praise."

God's Word is a lamp to your feet, a light to your way.

> Father,
> I do not want to embarrass you
> By the way I grieve.
> I want to honor you.
> May others see how great my
> God's strength is and
> Give you glory.

DAY 12

Normal Grief and Abnormal Grief

Erich Lindemann studied grief and found there can be distorted reactions and delayed reactions that may require you to seek professional help with your grieving. This does not mean you aren't strong enough but that attention to some aspect of your grief from a skilled person will help you get through unnecessarily deep or harmful suffering. He lists the following as signs that a griever needs help:

1. Acquisition of symptoms of the loved one's last illness.
2. Some new medical problems.
3. Severe changes in relationships with friends and relatives.
4. Furious hostility toward specific persons.
5. Self-destructive behavior or recurring thoughts of self-destruction.
6. Continuing depression.[1]

Remember, some of these criteria can, for a period, be considered normal. But do not hesitate to talk to your doctor or minister about anything that concerns you.

He Relieves Those Who Trust Him

Praise the LORD!

Praise the LORD, O my soul!
While I live I will praise the LORD;
I will sing praises to my God while I have my being.

Do not put your trust in princes,
Nor in a son of man, in whom there is no help.
His spirit departs, he returns to his earth;
In that very day his plans perish.

Happy is he who has the God of Jacob for his help,
Whose hope is in the LORD his God,
Who made heaven and earth,

The sea, and all that is in them;
Who keeps truth forever,
Who executes justice for the oppressed,
Who gives food to the hungry.
The LORD gives freedom to the prisoners.
The LORD opens the eyes of the blind;
The LORD raises those who are bowed down;
The LORD loves the righteous.
The LORD watches over the strangers;
He relieves the fatherless and widow;
But the way of the wicked He turns upside down.

The LORD shall reign forever—Your God, O Zion, to all
*   generations.*

Praise the LORD!

Psalm 146

The key word is *praise*. God is the source of life and its destination. Soon there definitely will be no more tears of grief. The psalmist tells you God is touched by your problems and tender to your needs. As long as you breathe you can praise him.

Remember, Jesus quoted from the psalms more than from other Scripture. He depended on them. He knew his Father was a very present help in trouble. He is your teacher and the example whom you can follow. Depend on the psalms for spiritual strength.

> Father, thank you.
> "Yet, despite all that happens
> To us, victory is ours through him
> Who loves us." This
> Is a lifeline for my soul
> Time after time.

DAY 13

Books That Are Easy to Read and Helpful to Those Who Grieve

1. *Good Grief*, by Granger E. Westberg (Philadelphia: Fortress Press, 1971). Available in large print, this short book, written in easy-to-understand language, a bestseller for years, provides understanding about ten stages of grief.
2. *A Grief Observed*, by C. S. Lewis (New York: Seabury Press, 1961). A beautiful, heartfelt book about Lewis's feelings in the loss of his spouse and his struggle for faith.
3. *The Will of God*, by Leslie D. Weatherhead (Nashville: Abingdon Press, 1972). Talks on the will of God that are especially meaningful to those in loss and sorrow.

If It Had Not Been the Lord

"If it had not been the LORD who was on our side,"
Let Israel now say—
"If it had not been the LORD who was on our side,
When men rose up against us,
Then they would have swallowed us alive,
When their wrath was kindled against us;
Then the waters would have overwhelmed us,
The stream would have gone over our soul;
Then the swollen waters
Would have gone over our soul."

Blessed be the LORD,
Who has not given us as prey to their teeth.
Our soul has escaped as a bird from the snare of the fowlers;
The snare is broken, and we have escaped.
Our help is in the name of the LORD,
Who made heaven and earth.

Psalm 124

This psalm presents a negative set of events only to dismiss their power because the Lord is present and is on the side of his people. God is for you, utterly committed to you. This truth helps you move from unstable anxiety to confident reassurance. God will not let you sink. He is all-powerful, on your side, and makes you victorious! When life doesn't seem to be a fair deal, you need reminders that God helps you to hold on. On many occasions I have said that if it had not been for the Lord I would have drowned in the turbulent waters of life's disappointments.

> God and Father,
> May your peace be
> In my heart and cover my ache.
> May I sleep in your arms tonight.

DAY 14

Using the Psalms Daily

Choose a psalm and read it a number of times so that some phrase can be carried on your lips through the day.

Think about the situation the psalmist may have been in and the intense feelings expressed by him, your brother in faith.

Identify this psalm as your prayer, your words, and your feelings being lifted to God.

Decide what God would have you do, if anything, as a result of your praying this psalm.

By doing this you unite with the covenant people of God and find him providing hope in times of despair.

Telling Yourself the Truth

As the deer pants for the water brooks,
So pants my soul for You, O God.
My soul thirsts for God, for the living God.
When shall I come and appear before God? . . .

Why are you cast down, O my soul?
And why are you disquieted within me?
Hope in God, for I shall yet praise Him
For the help of His countenance. . . .

Why are you cast down, O my soul?
And why are you disquieted within me?
Hope in God;
For I shall yet praise Him,
The help of my countenance and my God.

Psalm 42:1–2, 5, 11

These are the words of a person talking to himself, telling himself that how he feels is not as important as the truth about God. You may say it in words such as these:

> Father, that you are near to me,
> That I am in the great company of believers,
> That the name of Jesus Christ is the
> Name of the victor—all this reassures
> Me that I can and will endure,
> For you enable me to do so.
> You are present. That is enough for me!
>
> Lord, my mind swirls from this want and that.
> Yet, all I really want is a trusting faith.
> You are the God who provides;
> Your sufficiency is the reason for my joy.
> Give me the power to choose trust
> Today and every day.

DAY 15

Great Saints Faced Despair

Moses faced the dark night of his soul. Read Numbers 11:15.

Job cursed the day of his birth. Read Job 3:11–12.

Jeremiah felt the same way. Read Jeremiah 20:14–18.

Paul felt a deep groaning within himself. Read Romans 8:22–23.

Many of the saints felt as you may now feel: "I wish the Lord would take me. Why does he have me here?"

You are not alone.

God's Faithfulness

Show me Your ways, O Lord;
Teach me Your paths.
Lead me in Your truth and teach me,
For You are the God of my salvation;
On You I wait all the day.

Remember, O Lord, Your tender mercies and Your
*   lovingkindnesses,*
For they are from of old.
Do not remember the sins of my youth, nor my
*   transgressions;*
According to Your mercy remember me,
For Your goodness' sake, O Lord.

Psalm 25:4–7

The Hebrew word *hesed* (lovingkindness) speaks of God's steadfast love and is used frequently to emphasize the personal relationship God has with his people. He is true to his promises, constant in faithfulness, consistent in behavior. Knowing these things helps when you can only dimly see the purpose or timing of God in some event. This conviction can be yours: God is concerned about your condition and answers your cry in ways that sometimes surpass what you thought possible.

When grief covers God's gracious face, trust that, as Isaiah said, "those who wait on the LORD shall renew their strength; they shall mount up with wings like eagles, they shall run and not be weary, they shall walk and not faint" (Isa. 40:31). Waiting is very hard. Yet, the wait is rewarded.

> O Father,
> I'm thankful for your past kindness.
> I depend on your present strength.
> I praise you for your constant care
> And your attention to my pain.

DAY 16

Reaffirm the Center for Your Life

In the midst of uncertainty, reaffirming life's goal—pleasing God—helps to measure the value of your activities.

Possessions, power, and position fail to give a person significance.

People are not the hub of your life, although they are important. Other family members make "good spokes but weak hubs."

Jesus Christ is the way, the truth, and the life. He alone is life's center. "Come to me and you will have rest," he says.

Moments of Distress, Moments of Trust

But I am poor and sorrowful;
Let Your salvation, O God, set me up on high.
I will praise the name of God with a song,
And will magnify Him with thanksgiving.
This also shall please the LORD better than an ox or bull,
Which has horns and hooves.
The humble shall see this and be glad;
And you who seek God, your hearts shall live.
For the LORD hears the poor, and does not despise His
*   prisoners.*

Let heaven and earth praise Him,
The seas and everything that moves in them.

Psalm 69:29–34

Roland Murphy says in the powerful book *Out of the Depths: The Psalms Speak for Us Today* that we should be aware that psalmists who sought faith while their hearts fainted wrote lamentations over losses that could not be changed. They wrote laments to appeal to God's compassion to change their desperate situations.[1]

But their cries to God also often included some form of praise, some statement of confidence that God is faithful and that prayers are heard. When you alternate between notes of distress and moments of trust, you act as they did. Maybe that's why believers pray, "Lord, I believe; help thou my unbelief."

> Dear God,
> In my hour of grief help me
> Not to fear tomorrow.
> Let my house be restful
> To others who are weary.
> Let my ears willingly hear
> Another's painful story.
> Help me share my rest
> With other restless hearts.

DAY 17

Your Recovery Will Be Unique to You

Remember, your emotional pain is understood and accepted by God.

Be patient as you wait for God to provide the way of escape from pain. Likely it will be a process with a number of steps.

You will be given strength to accept reality without having to act as though you do not hurt.

Though hurt, you will continue to worship God. From him you have received everything good you have.

Do not blame yourself for not being better prepared or for being weak. Being human is not a sin.

Job Knows the Devastation of Grief

Then Job arose and tore his robe and shaved his head, and
he fell to the ground and worshiped. And he said:

"Naked I came from my mother's womb,
And naked shall I return there.
The LORD gave, and the LORD has taken away;
Blessed be the name of the LORD."

Job 1:20–21

In Job we meet a good man whose life is successful. Then Job's world caves in. He loses everything he has and everyone he dearly loves. No notice, no warning, just a "bolt from the blue." With some effort we can enter into his unspeakable grief. Yet we may forget that, because he chose faith, he can enter into your grief as a brother in this hour.

Job's actions seem strange. He tore the clothes he was wearing and shaved the hair from his head. He was crushed and did not pretend that it did not matter. No cover-up. But then he worshiped.

Chuck Swindoll says, "I am disappointed that someone, somewhere, many years ago, introduced the ridiculous idea that if you know the Lord, you do not grieve. That . . . you should not weep. With my whole heart, I disagree."[1] Job acknowledged God as his Lord at the moment of his devastation. Because we see his humility, he encourages us.

> Father,
> Though his times were long ago
> And his circumstances different,
> Allow me to find in Job
> A brother to my wounded spirit.

DAY 18

Let Another Person's Faith Stand with You

I believe the God of grace will strengthen and settle you.

I believe you will live, as your loved one would desire for you, beyond this time where all of life is overshadowed by this loss.

I believe you will see from a different frame of reference after a while.

Hard Pressed on Every Side

We are hard pressed on every side, yet not crushed; we are perplexed, but not in despair; persecuted, but not forsaken; struck down, but not destroyed—always carrying about in the body the dying of the Lord Jesus, that the life of Jesus also may be manifested in our body.

2 Corinthians 4:8–10

C. S. Lewis's honesty about his grief gives me courage and hope for mine. His *A Grief Observed* has helped those to whom I have recommended it. His line "I not only live each day in grief, but live each day thinking about living each day in grief" underscores the fresh fatigue grief often brings.

Like the indoor jogger on a treadmill, the painful loss runs in place over and over again. The thought, *Will it ever be different?* sinks the heart in fear. It is true that you will not "get over it"; it will always matter. But it will not always be a searing iron burning your spirit. The good news is that the pain will take its place in the heart's memory chamber as sweet sadness.

Father, help me seek your truth
and meaning in this time, trusting
that you will give life even
after this death.

DAY 19

The Truth about Partial Truths

"The gift of time will heal your grief." This is not entirely true. Time allows God to show you where this wound fits in your faith. Time itself resolves little. God is the healer, in his time.

"Get busy. The worst thing you can do is shut yourself away from people." Again, a partial truth. You need time for private grief. No one has a proper timetable for you. Healthy grieving, where God's strength is received, allows for regaining hope and recovering the sense of belonging with others that you need. A supportive friend will allow, even encourage, a time for you to be alone and a time to reenter life with other people.

"Life goes on. Whatever you do, do not drown in self-pity." The larger truth is that some self-pity is appropriate grieving. Self-pity, for a time, is not dangerous. You can feel marginalized (not taken seriously) when some well-intentioned friend warns against taking your loss too seriously. A lost relationship, never to be enjoyed again, is one of life's major losses.

Remember His Supper

The cup of blessing which we bless, is it not the communion of the blood of Christ? The bread which we break, is it not the communion of the body of Christ? For we, though many, are one bread and one body; for we all partake of that one bread.

1 Corinthians 10:16–17

Remember the Lord's Supper. You need it now. Why? Because in proclaiming the Lord's death until he comes, you renew the hope and promise that his death made certain. Taking the Supper, even with one other Christian, allows you to participate in a visible reminder of your being connected with him.

You proclaim by *action* the hope that right now you do not feel. The breaking of bread and drinking of the cup bring home to your broken heart the promise of God. It is unspeakably precious and is medicine to your soul. Many, in sorrow, shy away from this participation which so powerfully affirms hope.

Jesus is the Christ who was dead but is now alive forevermore (see Rev. 1:18). Many changes are being forced on you at present. Recall "the blood of the everlasting covenant" (Heb. 13:20). What *God has done*, remembered in the Supper, blesses your broken spirit. Let him feed you from his table.

> Christ, you are risen;
> Death is stripped of its power.
> Christ, you are risen;
> Death is robbed of its sting.
> Christ, you are risen;
> Glory be to your great name.

DAY 20

Solitude's Value

A creative solitude can bless grief recovery.

Solitude allows for reflection, active trust, and opening the heart for healing.

Jesus's all-night prayer on the mountain provided blessing from God (see Luke 6:12–13).

Solitude allows for journaling—jotting down notes that allow expression and reflection and often later result in increased understanding.

Death Will Not Have the Victory

So when this corruptible has put on incorruption, and this mortal has put on immortality, then shall be brought to pass the saying that is written: "Death is swallowed up in victory."

"O Death, where is your sting?
O Hades, where is your victory?"

The sting of death is sin, and the strength of sin is the law. But thanks be to God, who gives us the victory through our Lord Jesus Christ.

1 Corinthians 15:54–57

Henry Wadsworth Longfellow was right when he wrote that the grave is not the goal and return to dust was not spoken of the soul. You and I are only one step from our own deaths. But though inevitable, death will not triumph. Paul says that death is "the last enemy" but also that it will be defeated (see 1 Cor. 15:26).

Departure is sure. "To depart and be with Christ is far better" is a statement of magnificent hope in the midst of your terrible period of grief. These hours can be filled with indecision, uncertainty, and apprehension.

I am confident that God provides resources of strength from places you never imagined and balance and resilience that you presently think are not possible. He will. I know, because when you think "I'm so frail" is when he acts. Remember, there is no strong person. There are only persons made strong by God.

> Lord, I thank you.
> You have not abandoned me.
> You wipe my tears with your
> Ever-present, gentle hand.
> You called Lazarus from death to life.
> You are the life giver; in you I live
> Forever by our promise and
> Resurrection power.

DAY 21

The Horrible Pain

Because of my sickness, I know something about chronic pain. The pain of mourning a loved one is also a chronic, unrelenting pain.

You grieve with your whole being and often find yourself fatigued.

"How long will I feel this way?" you wonder. No one can tell you. Maybe you cried a lot at first and now you are just unmotivated and apathetic. You live with a painful emptiness; in fact, it may appear to be the worst emptiness anyone has ever experienced.

Some students of grief believe the full, aching pain usually lasts eighteen to twenty-four months, but that is really of little help to you right now.

What to Tell Your Friend

Be strong and of good courage, do not fear nor be afraid of them; for the LORD your God, He is the One who goes with you. He will not leave you nor forsake you.

Deuteronomy 31:6

Your friends mean well. One says you "will have to go through a cycle of grief work." They encourage you to cry and talk: "Don't suppress but express." If you don't "let it out," you're told, it comes out in harmful ways later. What are they really saying?

They want you to grieve in a healthy way so you can recover the desire to go forward. Why do their words sound so unreal and feel so unwanted? *Because you are not ready yet.* No one can grieve to a friend's expectation.

What should you do? Grieve in your own way. Thank everyone. Ask God to bless them. Then take one day at a time, or one hour if need be. Don't worry. You won't mess up. Grief is not a job performance.

Consider telling your friends, "I'm grieving, but I've never had to face a loss exactly like this. Stay close, but don't say too much unless I ask. I just want you to be a strong, mostly silent support system for me. I don't want to feel I'm losing my marbles. So help me, and somehow we'll make it through. I love you. You mean a lot to me. Just don't rush me, okay?"

> Father, may I follow Christ more closely today
> So that faith, trust, steadfastness, love,
> And, above all, hope will carry me
> Into tomorrow.

DAY 22

A Possible Strategy of Satan

Satan says, "If I can raise sustained anger toward God in the grieving, I will sense victory."

Satan says, "If I can sow a steady diet of doubt in a loving God and make grief engender bitterness and despair, I win."

Satan says, "If I enthrone loneliness so as to snuff out joy, I win."

Satan says, "If I can feed the griever's viewpoint that 'the meaningful part of my life is over,' I win."

Tell the Devil Off

Having disarmed principalities and powers, He made a public spectacle of them, triumphing over them in it.

Colossians 2:15

Tell yourself the truth about God's promises. Why now? Satan will say to you, "God doesn't care. God isn't here with you. God is busy with others." These are lies. Resist him and his lies fiercely (see 2 Cor. 2:11).

You will need God's armor. Remember, Satan's schemes are meant to separate you from God's love, but God will not let this happen. You can participate in holding on to his precious promises. Say out loud, "Satan, in the name of Jesus, get away from me. I know God's promises are true and his love is constant. I know God is for me." Don't make more of Satan's threat than of God's provisions.

Jesus Christ has won the decisive victory over Satan on the cross (see Col. 2:15). You are under the protection of the blood of Jesus. You are God's child. His Spirit lives in you. You may feel weak, but he is powerfully in you right now. Say with Paul, "Thanks be to God who always leads us in triumph in Christ" (2 Cor. 2:14). When Paul was weak, he gained his strength from God (see 2 Cor. 12). You will too!

> Lord, your kingdom
> Is within my heart
> And within my sight,
> A kingdom where no one will suffer loss.
> Lord Jesus, you alone are my hope.
> I give praise for the strength
> You have already given me.

DAY 23

No Condemnation or Judgment

You will not be given a passing or failing grade on how well you grieve, not by a really good friend.

You may not want to go out when asked by a friend, then feel isolated and forgotten later the same day that you said no. That is okay, because this is a time of confusion and uncertainty.

Be easy on yourself for feeling, at times, like a stranger to yourself. If you are forgetful, do not worry much; that goes with the grieving period. If your secret fear is that you are going crazy, relax; you are not.

Some who grieve say they have talked to their departed loved ones, dreamed about them, and even heard their voices. If these experiences enter into your period of grief, do not be concerned. These things are not surprising or alarming. Do not worry about them.

Your Future Is Bright

Do not fear any of those things which you are about to suffer. Indeed, the devil is about to throw some of you into prison, that you may be tested, and you will have tribulation ten days. Be faithful until death, and I will give you the crown of life.

Revelation 2:10

It is necessary to take only one day at a time through grief; otherwise the burden is too heavy. I promise you a day is coming: the coming again of your Lord Jesus Christ.

Peter writes of the morning star rising in your heart (see 2 Peter 1:19). You will see it. Do not shrink back in fear. Do not throw away your confidence. You do not have to quit. The battle is the Lord's, and his love has captured you.

We humans are inadequate, yet we say with Paul that our competence comes from God (see 2 Cor. 3:5–6). We are, through him, sons and daughters of the resurrection. Our hope is strengthened because we know the one in charge.

I do not underplay the pain of loss but emphasize the joy of God's future. Rest on the certainty of eternal victory in Jesus Christ.

Fitful nights, nagging worries, stabbing pangs of grief, and periods of loneliness become momentary troubles compared with an eternal weight of glory. You can survive now. The future is bright. Your faith is renewed from large reserves of God's promises.

> Dear God, O Father,
> Come and help me
> In this time of darkness.
> Keep the lamp of faith burning
> In my heart.

DAY 24

Do Not Judge Yourself

It is easy for you to say, "I am not handling this well." You are entitled to some down times. If you ask, "Am I going to make it?" this is normal.

Even anger is a normal reaction.

The pain will turn into sweet sadness.

Rebuilding in your life will take place even while memories of your loved one are strong. To accept is not to forget. You will not forget, ever!

The Need to Relinquish Control

And not only that, but we also glory in tribulations, knowing that tribulation produces perseverance; and perseverance, character; and character, hope. Now hope does not disappoint, because the love of God has been poured out in our hearts by the Holy Spirit who was given to us.

Romans 5:3–5

Norman Wright in *Recovering from the Losses of Life* says that loss traumatizes people so much because it carries with it the message, "You really are not in charge of your life." Loss of control is one of our most common fears. He quotes Lloyd Ogilvie who said, "A controller cannot trust God because he fears the control of his life resting in anyone's hands but his own."[1]

I believe Wright and Ogilvie have touched a sensitive nerve. Will you and I choose to live by faith, even in the terrible losses of our lives? God in his wisdom will do what is best; we know that. But will he do whatever we think is best? Probably not. I, for one, have not yet mastered the habit of resting in the wisdom of God for my life.

We must nudge each other closer to the source of comfort, the one we can trust: God our loving Father. He will direct. Ask him and expect him to do so.

> Lord of all wisdom and guidance,
> Big and small decisions face me.
> Help me make difficult choices;
> Help me do your will.
> Thank you for being beside me
> All the way.

DAY 25

Learning from the Darkness of Another

John Claypool's *Tracks of a Fellow Struggler* tells the story of his watching his young daughter, Laura Lae, die.

He was given patience, endurance, and strength in the midst of a despair that made him want to stop living.

He says, "If we are willing . . . we can become more grateful for the gifts we have been given, more open-handed in our handling of the events of life, more sensitive to the whole mysterious process of life, and more trusting in our adventure with God."[1]

Norman Wright: A Friend of Those Who Grieve

The eternal God is your refuge,
And underneath are the everlasting arms;
He will thrust out the enemy from before you,
And will say, "Destroy!"

Deuteronomy 33:27

Norman Wright's book *Recovering from the Losses of Life* is one I recommend for those who grieve.

First, he understands grief. He knows that grief forces you to sort through your needs and that it will be painful. He is a trustworthy guide. He is realistic about problems and adjustments.

Wright understands the loss of identity and shows how to evaluate usefulness and rediscover meaning. He suggests without demanding. You are likely to want to listen to this "good friend." He makes sense. He wisely points to Jesus: "None of us walks alone. Jesus Christ has been there and he is with us."[2]

Heavenly Father,
Calm my heart
And give me the compassion to reach
Out to others
Whose loneliness tears at their spirit.
Your name is peace to my heart.

DAY 26

Understanding Grief

Express your feelings about your loss, when you are ready, to one you trust.

Grief is cyclical: it comes up and grasps your throat. Then it goes down to the memory room of your heart.

Grief is natural and normal, though at times surprising to you. Grief has many faces. Its timing is its own.

He Touches Where You Hurt

When you pass through the waters, I will be with you;
And through the rivers, they shall not overflow you.
When you walk through the fire, you shall not be burned,
Nor shall the flame scorch you.
For I am the LORD your God,
The Holy One of Israel, your Savior;
I gave Egypt for your ransom,
Ethiopia and Seba in your place. . . .
Fear not, for I am with you;
I will bring your descendants from the east,
And gather you from the west.

Isaiah 43:2–3, 5

Canst thou not . . . pluck from the memory a rooted sorrow . . . which weighs upon the heart?

Shakespeare, *Macbeth*

Returning from visiting my neurosurgeon about a painful hip, these words came to my mind. Dr. Loyola had touched my hip in several places, saying, "Is here the most painful?" until he found just the spot. More than just finding the spot, he knew what to do to ease the pain.

Jesus knows how to get inside your hurt and apply the truth about his Father that truly comforts. I like David Larson's emphasis that "Christ can heal and Christ can help."[1] With God nothing is impossible (see Luke 1:37).

> Father, thank you for knowing I cannot
> Bear this grief alone.
> Others try but they cannot
> Keep my faith from stumbling;
> Only you can.
> Carry me gently
> Through the days and nights.

DAY 27

Getting through Grief

You will know you are getting through the grief when certain things happen:

You realize that this loss will always be a part of you.

You accept the fact that you cannot change what happened.

You know you can live with the memory but with less pain, later, by the grace of God.

You are the same person, but in some ways you have grown; however, thankfully you will never forget.

Facing your pain is mostly between you, a good friend, and God.

The pain of your loss is uniquely personal, but you sense that the Lord understands.

A Patience Filled with Hope

Now hope does not disappoint, because the love of God has been poured out in our hearts by the Holy Spirit who was given to us.

Romans 5:5

Stanley Hauerwas in *The Peaceable Kingdom* says that "there is no cure for deceptions and illusions concerning our own strength. . . . Our hope is in the God whom we believe has already determined the end of history, in the cross and resurrection of Jesus Christ."[1] This is why we are patient in tragic events and why we don't abandon people when bad things happen to them.

Our joy is in our trust. This life is marked by frequent losses, but loss is not the *final* event. We know a good

God. We learn to wait, to be at rest with ourselves, to enjoy God's offer of peace.

Do not worry that you are "wasting time" or "not accomplishing anything." Tell of God's kindness to you. You are loved by him now, although you feel helpless. God's people are faithful when they tell each other that they are loved by their heavenly Father. Give him credit for your survival.

> Father, in the midst of my grief
> I confess your goodness.
> I desire one thing only:
> To be close to you forever.

DAY 28

Four Paths That Delay Grief

Denying does not ease the pain of your grief, whether you deny feelings or act like nothing has happened.

Minimizing your need to grieve does not ease the pain.

Idealizing the one you lost does not help. Telling the truth about the good and bad in that person's life is all that frees you to move toward recovery.

Retreating to another time in memory only delays grief. The way to the goal is straight ahead.

Giving Meaning to Grief

> *He died for all, that those who live should live no longer for themselves, but for Him who died for them and rose again.*
>
> 2 Corinthians 5:15

Paul Welter, an insightful Christian counselor, writes that "meaning" refers to the significance we attach to our existence and that the lack of such meaning can be devastating. People are born with some kind of innate equipment that yearns for human connection. Death severs the connection that has been established, forcing the disconnected to grapple with meaninglessness.

That's why those who counsel often hear, "I felt I had lost a part of myself that brought sunshine to my life."[1] Feeling that a part of the self is missing explains or gives meaning to grief. Dr. Welter encourages you to place the meaning on grief that will best help you live out the purpose you have given your life.

Psychiatrist Victor Frankl, a brilliant young doctor, was held prisoner in a concentration camp during World War II. While there he learned and helped other prisoners learn the value of attitudinal change—that it didn't matter what they expected from life, but rather what life expected from them.[2] Ask yourself, *What meaning (that will assist me to fulfill good life goals) will I place on this loss?* Christ provides useful answers.

> Lord, I am tired of saying good-bye.
> The changes I witness
> Make me afraid.
> Thank you that Christ
> Announced that
> The final word is life.
> I long for heaven where
> There are no good-byes.

DAY 29

The Intensity of Grief

You cry, feel empty, but continue to function. But normal grief has not one beginning and one ending point. It is cyclical. It ebbs and flows, gains intensity and slacks off.

Beware of timetables. "It will take one year," she says. "Experts tell us you must pass through eight seasons (two years)," another offers. You'll be "over it in _____" or feeling "almost back to normal in _____." You will recover is the truth, but the time is in God's hands. No one knows for sure when.

Persistent physical symptoms require a careful look from a competent, concerned doctor: panic attacks, continual stomachaches, headaches, feelings or actions that indicate nagging depression, or sleep problems that lead to constant exhaustion. Use common sense. Also, listen to those who love you. It's wise to check things out.

Assurance over Fear

> What then shall we say to these things? If God is for us, who
>   can be against us? He who did not spare His own Son,
>   but delivered Him up for us all, how shall He not with
>   Him also freely give us all things?

Romans 8:31–32

Eugenia Price won my heart when she wrote *What Really Matters* and concluded that five words hold the key: *If God is for us.* She has found the key to a trusting heart in a time of terrible loss. In the inside cover of my New Testament I have written down reassuring truths about God. One is 1 Corinthians 3:21–23:

God has already given you everything you need. . . .
He has given you the whole world to use, and life and
even death are your servants. He has given you all of
the present and all of the future. All are yours, and
you belong to Christ, and Christ is God's (TLB).

I suspect that we underestimate the power of the lies
that Satan tells. Knowing that feelings are as unpredict-
able as a carnival roller coaster, I find it helpful to go
back to my anchor: Scripture—those places marked in
my Bible that are safe havens in a storm-filled period
of life.

> Lord,
> When relationships
> Are broken by death, I am reminded
> That only in you do
> I find life everlasting.
> Your name brings me comfort and peace.
> I long to see you, Lord.
> Then I'll find my final rest.

DAY 30

What to Do with Time?

Your responsibility is to face the time at hand. "Each day has trouble enough."

Times of memories that cut to the quick are necessary for healing.

There is strength within this promise from God: "I will be in this moment with you, so of course expect me in the next hour. I'll be there."

Time is not a problem; it is the arena in which God does his perfect work.

Jesus's time at the tomb of Lazarus allowed Mary and Martha to know that he cared. He cries with you today.

Anticipate. You will reach the journey's destination. Time will no longer hold you in the tension caused by sorrow.

Freshness of Hope

Remember my affliction and roaming,
The wormwood and the gall. . . .
This I recall to my mind,
Therefore I have hope.

Through the LORD's mercies we are not consumed,
Because His compassions fail not.
They are new every morning;
Great is Your faithfulness.

Lamentations 3:19, 21–23

Why would anyone read the book of Lamentations? "Just a series of heartbroken cries" one writer calls it. Maybe in the presence of human misery everyone needs reminders that sorrow is a permanent part of the fabric of life. But when the misery is inside you, you want to run from such writings. Don't do it. You must live through, not avoid. Nothing in life lasts forever. In the end your grip grows loose on your best treasures. One grieving person wrote me this:

> I'm aware of being an embarrassment to everyone I meet. . . . Perhaps the bereaved ought to be isolated in special settlements like lepers. This change is the one for which no training was available. We as part of the family of men are characterized by the fact we bury those we love. We cry for others, with others, and for ourselves. In the midst of these changes, run to the one who is constant, the one with new resources of strength every day.

> Lord, I better understand that this world
> Is filled with sorrow.
> Thank you for
> Saving this world.
> We love and lose.
> You, not this world,
> Are our home.
> I praise you for teaching me
> Through my sorrow to trust you.

CONCLUSION

You have lost a treasured, dearly loved person. You face many difficult tests because of your grief. Maybe you feel alone. I want to be with you as a brother. I want to bear your burden (see Gal. 6:2) and seek to move alongside you with words of comfort. I am aware that only God is the great Comforter. I believe he, in the power of the Holy Spirit, will fill the void in your life. Do not listen to the devil's lie that your meaningful life has ended. Your God says it is not so. I like the following words of Martin Luther:

> The Lord our God is a God of the humble and perplexed hearts, who are in need, tribulation and danger. If we were strong, we would be proud and haughty. God shows his power in our weakness.[1]

In the strength God provides you will survive. You will comfort others who grieve. You will in your own way and in God's good time be a healer of broken hearts. God bless you.

Appendix 1

A Letter to Becky's Father

My life and work is such that daily I am given the opportunity to see into the hearts of others. Often I feel inadequate to meet their needs, but always I am confident that God has no inadequacies and that if I can point these hurting hearts to him they will find the way to healing.

But Becky's father is different.

Becky's father wrote me searching for lost hope. His letter touched my heart deeply. Because of his letter I see and appreciate my beautiful, healthy daughters more intensely. I want to help him, to share with him God's love.

Dear Randy,

Since I lost my daughter my heart is as close to being broken and still alive as possible. We had gone through thirteen years of chemotherapy for leukemia, had two remissions, and finally lost Becky to pneumonia. Becky was seventeen when she died, a junior in high school and a member of the honor society. She was our only child, and we couldn't have had a happier and fuller relationship.

Since her death I have not been able to make any sense out of all of this and I'm surprised at how weak my faith is. I've seen so much suffering of innocent children for so many years that the image of a loving God is too much for me to accept any longer. Becky suffered for so long that I can't comprehend anything that could justify this kind of existence. It's not enough to be told only, "You have to have faith." I think I deserve more.

I miss my Becky so much sometimes I don't know which way is up. I know my wife feels the same. We keep very busy, and that allows us to go on day after day. But I keep expecting something to change. So far, happiness is still gone, and we only become harder instead of more accepting.

My attendance at a support group for bereaved parents helps, but I'm still looking for some strong understanding to

allow me to accept this lousy situation.
I know I sound like some spoiled crybaby
and I really don't care, because I have
to have a better way of living with this
than I have right now.

I would really like to be able to
lean on my faith so much more than I can
right now, but I really don't expect
anything now after how abandoned I feel
by my God. I have prayed so much so many
times for mercy for Becky. I looked hard
and saw so little. How I wish I would
have seen more. I am hurt really badly
and don't expect to understand soon. But
I still seem to want to keep trying.

Signed: A brokenhearted father

The letter reminds me of Francis Thompson's *The Hound of Heaven*. It's about God's pursuit of a reluctant soul. This father sounds as though he considers abandoning faith; but I think God won't let him go. He talks about feeling "abandoned . . . by my God" and how he keeps trying to understand. It may help him to understand that his preoccupation with trying to understand is an indication that God has not abandoned him. God is trying to draw him near.

I think God cries too over a letter like this. After all, God *made* Becky. He knows her better than her father does, and he loves her more, so it must have been anguish for him to watch Satan attack her. Artists love what they make. If somebody comes along and ruins the creation, they grieve. God must be even more attached to his living works of art.

God is crying with this father. But God has demonstrated his care by doing more than shed tears. He gave a Son to die willingly to defeat the power of sin and death. The final word is not *death*, but because of God, the final word is *life*.

I think too that this father grieves over his loss of faith that had all the answers, his lost worldview where the good guys won. That's in addition to his grief over his daughter.

I want to share with you a letter I wrote Becky's father. I sought to respond to one whose heart is broken:

    I read your letter when it first came
    and I have read it several times in
    the days since. It is powerful and has
    powerfully moved my life as it opens a
    window into your world and the heaviness
    of your heart.

    I have wept and been thankful all
    at the same time. I am thankful that
    you are a skillful communicator and a
    genuine human being with great capacity
    for joy as well as sorrow. I rejoice in
    the life which Becky lived. She was the
    center of your joy, for sure.

    I know a little about grief, though
    no one really understands another
    person's grief. And I don't understand
    yours except perhaps by a flicker. My
    heart goes out to you in gratitude that
    you are honest with your feelings. God
    understands and respects that. Your
    letter didn't disturb me; rather, it
    tells me some matters go deeply into the
    soul.

You are in touch with your feelings and with the harshness of suffering in the world. Beyond that, you have the capacity and willingness to be in touch with a God whose nature is loving.

There are really two choices for you as you respond to Becky's death. The first is bitterness and despair, taking that hollow place in the marrow of your bones and looking at it only as darkness, with no meaning and no possibility of providing light or hope to any other human being.

Another choice is available. You can press toward life with the decision to love and to serve others as a "wounded healer," someone who has been significantly hurt and who uses that understanding to move close to other people in their own pain so that they do not feel alone. You can serve those who hurt because you understand their pain.

I know a little bit about this second choice because I was diagnosed with a life-threatening illness at the age of twenty-nine. I had three children under four years of age. I've seen some of the darker side of life and I would be among the first to say that life is not easy. In fact, I would quickly say that it hurts badly.

But I would add that life is a gift from God. He's the only one I've found who has shoulders big enough to bear the losses, broken lives, and shattered dreams. I've looked for permanent promises in broken people, but the promise of meaning for my life I have found from God, my Father.

When I ask, "Where is God when it hurts?" I find the best answer is in his own suffering, the giving of his own Son (I speak here of Jesus's death on the cross). His death speaks to all human suffering. It is a raw decision of faith to select him. But it is a life-giving choice rather than a death-dealing choice. I believe that love is stronger than death. *Jesus's love means that Becky's death is not the final word about Becky.*

I'm sure you understand some of these things better than I do. All that I have experienced about Jesus teaches me to trust God with all that I have found difficult to understand about suffering and death.

Appendix 2

Preparing for the Holidays

Some days you never forget, especially days of great joy and satisfaction, or days of enormous pain and sorrow.

Thanksgiving Day, 1973, is one of those memorable days of pain in my life. I was a cancer patient lying in the bed of a large cancer hospital. My mind was filled with doubts and fears, but worst of all, I couldn't be with my dear wife and three lovely children.

August 5, 1977, is another unforgettable day. I said good-bye to my mother, age fifty-seven, after her seven long years of illness. She was the center of all holidays in our family. Her touch made them very special. No holiday since has been the same. Does anyone begin to understand the empty feeling, the sorrow no words can express?

Do you wonder as the holiday season approaches, the first one since you lost your special someone, how you will survive? For some time now I've counseled those who grieve and have learned that no one thing works for everyone. Perhaps nothing will help ease the pain right now. Even God (who, you know, cares) seems distant. If that's true, if that's how dark it is right now, then I pray that God will give you the special strength and care you need.

But let me gently urge you to read on a little further. I care about you. Maybe one thought here will bless you. I hope so.

I want to give some suggestions for coping with the holidays this year. Of course, I know there are no easy answers as you struggle with the pain. But those who grieve have often mentioned the following principles to me, and maybe they will help you a little.

1. You will want to expect this time to be hard. But you will survive. I do not say holidays will be happy. I do not say this time will be anything but difficult. You have never had to do this before, but you can do a better job of coping if you expect some things to be hard.

2. I ask you to be easy on yourself. Some of the struggle of going through a difficult loss is not just finding the strength to get through the loss but how hard you are on yourself. You expect a superhuman strength that, when the chips are down, you likely won't have. Then you will become very critical and sometimes even destructive toward yourself.

Why shouldn't you be content while you honestly accept your weakness? You who leave a crowded room to cry alone, I'd like you to consider staying with the people. They need to know that grief is part of the real world. You may think, "I've got a child. I have to be strong for him." You've put a burden on yourself that's pretty incredible. How about just being honest with him? Are you going to teach him to fake it till he makes it, or is it better to be his model: "This hurts, son"? If someone could give you the gift of being gentler with yourself, you would do better.

3. You need to summon all the emotional support, spiritual support, and good mental health principles you can. Don't be afraid to ask for help. You're not self-sufficient. Ask one friend, "If I get down, may I call and talk with you? Will you keep my calls confidential—just between you and me?" Then use that friend for a safety valve.

I made this request of a friend. At two o'clock one morning I called him because of my fears. I asked him, "Remember, I asked if I could call you? I need to talk to you." He said, "Start talking. I'll wake up on the third or fourth sentence. But I'm glad you called." He saved my life that night.

4. Don't be afraid to enjoy something or somebody. It's okay to enjoy something. It's okay to enjoy somebody. A widow once told me of her survival technique for social occasions. Before attending any gathering she would say to herself, "I'm going to give these people the gift of enjoying themselves. And I'm going to try to watch them enjoy themselves, and that will be enough for me."

When you grieve you work to accept the reality and experience the pain of adjusting to the environment without the person who has died. After time you finally begin to withdraw the emotional investment you had in that person who is no longer present. You may someday reinvest it. Most people are slow to reinvest, by the way, because they believe it dishonors the memory of the one they loved. But eventually they come to a point where they say, "When I do this, I'm not dishonoring his or her memory." This is healthy grief that finally, *on your timetable*, allows you to reinvest yourself in your own life and future.

5. Draw on your faith and tell God exactly how you feel. During your period of grief, some who have a strong faith are going to be embarrassed over your feelings toward God. One widow told me, "I told God I was so mad at him for letting my husband pass away on Christmas day." You can be angry at God and tell him all about it. It's okay. He understands. He wants you to bring him your grief.

6. This requires the greatest strength of all: be gentle with your consolers. They don't know what to do or say. But they are going to do something and say something. Just forgive them. Give them needed but undeserved kindness. The worst are the ones who think they know what to do and say. You are going to have to grant them double forgiveness.

7. A very important principle of mental health is to do something out of love for somebody, not out of duty or expectation: buying Christmas gifts for the grandchildren, sending a birthday card to your

aunt. You will enjoy a marvelous feeling that you are a worthwhile person when you do something out of love for someone else. You will want to do this not only because of their need but also more because of your need.

8. Try not to withdraw. Let friends include you. If you receive three invitations for social activities, try to take at least one. And you can say, "This will be hard for me. But, yes, I'll come. Would you be willing for me not to stay the whole time?" Try to push yourself out a little bit. It's a mentally healthy thing to do.

9. I know this is painful for you, but let the past memories flood you. It is genuinely human to do that. You and I are a part of everything that has ever hurt us, and it's a permanent part of us. I have a massive scar on my hand where I went through a window at the age of twelve. It reminds me of the four and one-half hours the doctors needed to sew my hand back together. That scar is a part of me. That experience of insecurity is a permanent memory. Now, the good news it that good experiences, times of joy, are also in our memory banks. Let those past memories flood you.

10. Draw strength and hope from your faith. You decided long ago to trust a God who cares. You can call on that faith to help see you through. You must repeat these faith statements from conviction, for you are not always going to feel them emotionally. I have said things that are true when many times I did not feel them.

I believe God has done something that has forever changed the face of human suffering: He raised his Son from the dead. If you believe that, now is the time to restate it. Your God cares.

11. Visit the graveside and talk. Or take a favorite picture from that album in the closet and talk and cry. It may be on the anniversary of the time you lost him or her that you need to set aside a two-hour period to go to walk and talk in that graveyard. Don't say, "That's too painful." There is something healthy for you when you walk toward your pain, so you will want to let the reality be with you.

    George Burns said that he would go and talk to Gracie. She was the love of his life. He sat once every two weeks at Forest Lawn Cemetery and talked to her about what he was doing. That was one of the smartest things George ever did. He was a healthy guy.

    Feel free to apologize to your loved one if you carry some regret about how you failed him. You can forgive him for not being all he could have been. Just tell him good-bye. You can even forgive him for leaving. People who talk to those they love and lose may be smarter or healthier than the rest of us.

12. I started by saying, "Expect this time to be hard, but you will survive," and I want to conclude with, "Remember that you are normal." Dr. Joseph Worden says it will take at least four seasons, one full year, to make significant progress in dealing with your loss, and maybe two or three years. I notice many make the mistake of putting a timetable on grief. Nobody can tell you how long it will take you to reach that healthy level of coping. We are all different. Your task is to work from the ache

to sweet sadness. The good news is that you are likely to get there. Why do I believe that? Well, I like the Old Testament reference to God as our strength and refuge, "a very present help in time of trouble." He will get you there.

NOTES

Preface

1. C. W. Brister, *Pastoral Care in the Church* (New York: HarperCollins, 1992), 254.

2. Lawrence Crabb and Dan Allender, *Encouragement: The Key to Caring* (Grand Rapids: Zondervan, 1984), 15.

Chapter 1: It's Okay to Cry

1. Lawrence E. Holst, ed., *Hospital Ministry, The Role of the Chaplain Today* (New York: Crossroad Publishing Company, 1991), 144.

Chapter 3: Make a New and Special Friendship

1. Norman Wright, *Recovering from the Losses of Life* (Old Tappan, NJ: Revell, 1991), 77.

Day 2: Grief Complications You Can Avoid

1. Eugenia Price, *Getting Through the Night* (New York: Dial Press, 1982), 27.

Day 3: When Is It Time to Cry?

1. David Redding, *Psalms of David* (Westwood, NJ: Revell, 1963), 45.

Day 4: Other Grievers Teach Us

1. Earl Grollman, *What Helped Me When My Loved One Died* (Boston: Beacon Press, 1982).

Day 5: Facing Your Own Death

1. David A. Crenshaw, *Bereavement: Counseling the Grieving Throughout the Life Cycle* (New York: Continuum Publishing Co., 1990).

Day 9: Your Special Needs

1. David K. Switzer, "The Crisis of Grief," in *The Minister As Crisis Counselor* (Nashville: Abingdon, 1986), 143–74.

Day 11: Knowing What Sorrow Means

1. Edgar Jackson, *When Someone Dies* (Philadelphia: Fortress Press, 1971), 11.

Day 12: Normal Grief and Abnormal Grief

1. As listed by Alan Wolfelt, *Death and Grief: A Guide for Clergy* (Muncie, IN: ADI, Inc., 1988), 89.

Day 16: Reaffirm the Center for Your Life

1. Bernhard W. Anderson, ed., *Out of the Depths: The Psalms Speak for Us Today* (Philadelphia: Westminster, 1983), 77.

Day 17: Your Recovery Will Be Unique to You

1. Charles Swindoll, *The Strong Family* (Portland, OR: Multnomah, 1991), 195.

Day 24: Do Not Judge Yourself

1. Wright, *Recovering*, 33–34.

Day 25: Learning from the Darkness of Another

1. John Claypool, *Tracks of a Fellow Struggler* (Dallas: Word, 1974), 103.

2. Wright, *Recovering*, 203.

Day 26: Understanding Grief

1. David L. Larson, *Caring for the Flock* (Wheaton: Crossway, 1991), 87.

Day 27: Getting through Grief

1. Stanley Hauerwas, *The Peaceable Kingdom* (Notre Dame, IN: University of Notre Dame Press, 1983), 144–45.

Day 28: Four Paths That Delay Grief

1. Paul Welter, *Counseling and the Search for Meaning* (Waco: Word Books, 1987), 90.
2. Ibid., 53.

Conclusion

1. T. S. Kepler, ed., *Table Talk of Martin Luther* (Waco: Word Publishing, 1952), 285.

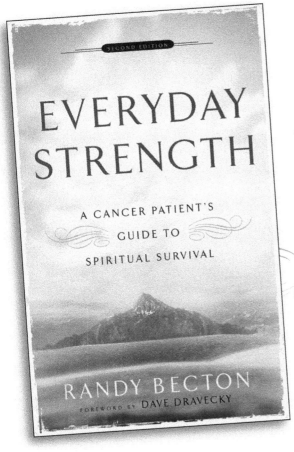